TOUCHING THE CLOAK

BIBLICAL MONOLOGUES BASED ON THE ENCOUNTERS OF JESUS

by Jackie Mouradian

Touching the Cloak

Written by Jackie Mouradian
Illustrated by Bill Crooks
Graphic design by Noble Design

Mosaic Creative

www.mosaiccreative.co.uk
info@mosaiccreative.co.uk
+44 (0) 118 9611359
First edition 2014

ISBN #: 9781326108953

Mosaic Creative are committed to using the visual and performing arts in providing accessible training and resources for the voluntary sector in the UK and overseas.

Contents

1   Introduction

5   Monologues

6   The woman who touched the cloak of Jesus
9   The woman who touched the cloak and Jairus (back to back)
13   The woman at the well
16   Bartimaeus
19   Up on the roof
23   The widow of Nain
26   Zacchaeus
30   The woman caught in adultery
33   The feeding of the 5000
37   Peter walks on water
40   Peter and Andrew (back to back)

45   Monologues For Holy Week and Easter

46   Mary makes bread
48   Mary and the mother of the thief (back to back)
51   Martha and Mary (back to back)
54   Judas
56   Mary at the cross
58   The Thief on the Cross
61   Mary Magdalene at the tomb
64   Thomas
68   Breakfast on the beach

Introduction

The Bible is full of fantastic stories of transformation, particularly those stories of the people Jesus encountered in his three year ministry. In scripture, these stories are written in a factual way and emotions are rarely visited even though the lives of the people involved were changed forever. It is up to the reader to imagine what those emotions might be. Through drama we can present the thoughts, feelings and emotions of the various characters and experience the stories in a new way.

Drama is a passion of mine. It appeals to all our senses and emotions and I have used it both in my church life and in my work in community development to bring familiar Bible stories to life. There are many forms of drama, but my favourite is the monologue. In a drama sketch, the feelings of the characters can be inferred from their conversations but in a monologue, a character can tell us their story, recall conversations and express their feelings and opinions directly to the audience.

The monologues in this book are the voices of those who encountered Jesus. Some knew him well, others just met him once, but for all, their time with Jesus was transformational. The way Jesus interacted with them gives us insights into how we as individuals and as a church can be transformational in our own communities.

Several of the stories told in these monologues involve those people on the outskirts of society – the poor, the marginalised, the stigmatised. I have had the privilege of seeing these monologues performed in the course of my work both here and overseas, in different cultures and different languages. Bringing the words on the page to life in this way has helped church members empathise and identify with the characters Jesus encountered and this has played a huge part

in raising awareness of the role of the church in community particularly to be there for the poor and marginalised.

The title of this book takes its name from one of the first monologues I wrote – the story of the woman who touched the cloak of Jesus. Writing this script caused me to wonder what it must have been like for Jairus, waiting while Jesus gave time and space to this woman, knowing his daughter was dying. This led me to write what I call a 'back to back' monologue, in which we hear two people's version of the same events – the woman and Jairus. This is also included in this collection along with 3 other back to back monologues featuring Peter and Andrew, Mary and the mother of the thief on the cross and Martha and Mary of Bethany.

Towards the end of the book, I have included some monologues that would be suitable to use during Holy week and Easter.

However you use these monologues, whether in a church service, a Bible study, training course, or dramatic production, I hope you enjoy them.

Tips for performing the monologues

Many of these monologues are on the lengthy side so it may seem daunting to think about learning the words, but I would encourage you to do so. Talking to the audience or congregation directly without a script will have the effect of grabbing the attention. Also with a monologue it doesn't matter so much if you don't stick to the exact words – no one else is relying on your cue, so as long as you get the essence of the story and the feelings involved, you can afford to stray off script occasionally.

When learning the script, read it through several times to start with to get an overall feel for it and the character, and then start learning paragraph by paragraph. The key to performing well is to be really inside your character. Who are they? Where have they come from ? What is the motivation for their words and actions? The more you are under the skin of the character, the better your portrayal will be. When performing, choose an article of clothing or a prop that will help you portray the character, maybe a shawl for the woman who touched the cloak, or a water jug for the woman at the well.

Of course, another advantage of performing a script rather than reading it is that you have freedom of movement. You can move about as you feel led. Adding movements to the performance can also help with the line learning as you will associate certain lines with certain movements.

Tips for reading the monologues

Of course, sometimes there will not be time to learn a monologue, and in this case a dramatised reading is a good second best. The first rule of reading a script rather than learning it by heart is never try to cover up the fact that you are reading it. Be up front about it – your audience won't mind if you present the script in a dramatic and engaging way.

When preparing for the reading, read through the script many times as you would if you were learning it. This will help you become your character and you will become familiar with the piece. This will allow you to look up occasionally to make eye contact with your audience without fear of losing your place. One advantage reading has over learning a script is that you will not have those anxious fears of forgetting the next line and this will help you deliver the words with confidence and feeling.

Always practise your reading aloud. Facial expression and posture can also help in your portrayal of the feelings of your character, so use them. It would be a good idea to have the monologue printed out in large enough print for easy reading from a lectern and try to have all the pages visible so there is no need for turning and rustling of paper.

Tips for performing back to back monologues

Divide your performance area into two halves and each character works within their own half. They certainly do not need to be back to back but they do not interact with each other even though there is a relationship between the lines they are saying. Make sure you get the pace right. These scripts are written in a way that there is a link between the words each are saying, so they work best if they are performed at a good pace. So even though there is no need to memorise the script of the other character, it is important to know the cues very well. If the script is to be read rather than performed, then have two lecterns and the readers should address the audience rather than each other.

Finally

Whether you are performing by heart or reading the script it is a good idea to have someone with you when you rehearse to give constructive criticism and encouragement. Also, whenever possible, ask someone to read the relevant passage from the Bible before the monologue is performed.

MONOLOGUES

THE WOMAN WHO TOUCHED THE CLOAK OF JESUS

LUKE 8: 40- 56

She came up behind him and touched the edge of his cloak,
and immediately her bleeding stopped.

Martha, my neighbour, has just been in to see me. She was so excited,

"Have you heard about Jairus?" she said. "Have you heard? His little girl died, she actually died and Jesus raised her from the dead! Can you believe that? He raised her from the dead!"

Then she was gone, dear Martha, off to tell someone else the good news.

Can I believe it? Yes, I can believe it. He's done it before. You see, I know a lot about Jesus. Stuck inside my house, shunned by everyone, this is what has kept me going- listening to the people standing outside the window in the street. And often they talk of Jesus. He's done such amazing things. He healed a leper, a demon-possessed man, a centurion's servant who was close to death and yes, in Nain, he brought back to life the only son of a poor widow. Jesus seems to care about everyone; lepers, mad men, widows, even centurions. So when I saw him from my window, coming through our village, I just thought he might care about me.

It's been so lonely having this illness. Twelve years I've been suffering, twelve years I've been bleeding. No-one has been able to heal me. I've spent all my money on doctors and instead of getting better I've just been getting worse. But the worst thing is there has been no-one to share this suffering with. No-one has come near me. I was unclean. Not acceptable. Who in their right mind would come near me? Martha would come by occasionally and leave me food, but she didn't stay. Why should she? So I was left on my own- just waiting to die.

And then, there he was, Jesus, walking through the village. I heard the crowds at first, and then I heard his name. So I went to the window and looked out. A huge crowd of people was there. I recognised a few. Jairus, the leader of the synagogue, was there. He looked desperate and as they came closer I could hear what he was saying,

"My daughter, my daughter, please heal my daughter!" over and over again.

He was out of his mind with worry. Ah, so that's where Jesus was going. This was important and I didn't want to stop him, but I was desperate too, and I thought that if I could just touch him as he walked by, that would be enough. He could heal me. But how? Such a big crowd.

But somehow I had to do it. So I stepped out of my house. Some people shouted at me to stay away, to get back indoors, away from decent people. For once I didn't listen; I kept going into the crowd, closer and closer to Jesus. But I couldn't get close enough – there were just too many people, and I wasn't strong enough to push my way through them. I could feel my excitement turning into despair, but then I looked down, and there it was – the edge of his cloak right in front of me, trailing along the ground. I leant forward and reached out my arm as far as I could, and then I felt it. I felt the material brush past my fingers. And then the most amazing feeling. I can't describe it, but it swept through the whole of my body and I knew, I just knew I was healed.

I tried to make my way out of the crowd, but then Jesus stopped.

"Who touched me?" he said.

One of his friends said, "There's a crowd of people all round you, what do you mean?" I breathed a sigh and looked for a way out of the crowd. But Jesus didn't move; he spoke again.

"Someone touched me. Power has gone from me."

Well, I knew I had to own up. So I fell at his feet and told him it was me, and I told him why I had been so desperate to touch his clothes; those twelve years, the shame. Everyone was listening to me now, including people who had ignored and avoided me for years. Now they knew what that had been like for me. And then I looked up at Jesus. He was smiling. Such warmth in his eyes. Then he said to me the words I will never forget as long as I live.

"Daughter, your faith has healed you. Go in peace."

"Daughter, go in peace."

Later on that day he gave a little girl her life back. I think he knew he'd done the same for me.

THE WOMAN WHO TOUCHED THE CLOAK OF JESUS & JAIRUS

(BACK TO BACK)

LUKE 8: 40- 56

"Don't be afraid; just believe, and she will be healed"

Voice one: The woman who touched the cloak
Voice two: Jairus

Martha, my neighbour, has just been in to see me – she was so excited. "You'll never believe it," she said. "The little girl – Jairus's daughter – she died, she actually died, and Jesus raised her from the dead! Can you believe it? Can you believe he actually did that?" Then she was gone, dear Martha, off to tell someone else the good news.

Can I believe it? Yes I can believe it. He's done it before. You see, I know a lot about Jesus. Stuck inside my house, shunned by everyone, this is what has kept me going- listening to people outside the window, talking. And they talk a lot about Jesus.

I know a lot about Jesus. He's done some amazing things. I've seen him at the synagogue teaching with such authority. There are other religious leaders who seem to hate him but I can't understand that. It all seems to make perfect sense when he speaks. And he doesn't just speak, he heals people. He changes lives with just with a word or a touch, casting out demons, healing physical deformities.

He healed a leper, a demon-possessed man, a centurion's servant who was close to death and yes, in Nain, he raised to life the only son of a poor widow.

How I longed for my daughter to feel that healing touch. She was so sick. I knew she was dying. This man was my only hope. If only he would come to my daughter, my beautiful daughter, just twelve years old.

Twelve years I've been suffering with this illness, twelve years I've been bleeding. No-one has been able to heal me. I've spent all my money on doctors and instead of getting better I've just been getting worse. And the worst thing is there has been no-one to share this suffering with. No-one has come near me. I was unclean. Not acceptable. Who in their right mind would come near me? Martha would come by occasionally and leave me food, but she didn't stay – why should she? So I was left on my own- just waiting to die.

And then like an answer to prayer, there he was - Jesus in our village. A large crowd had gathered to welcome him. I had to take this opportunity so I ran to meet him and then in front of the crowd I fell on my knees before him and begged him to come to my house. "Please master," I cried out, "please come, my daughter is dying – please come and heal my daughter." "Yes," he said, "show me the way."

And then, there he was, walking through the village. I heard the crowds at first, and then I heard his name. I went to the window and looked out. A huge crowd of people were there. I recognised a few. Jairus, the leader of the synagogue, was there. He looked desperate and as they came closer I could hear what he was saying, "My daughter, my daughter – please heal my daughter!" over and over again. He was out of his mind with worry. Ah, so that's where Jesus was going. This was important and I didn't want to stop him, but I was desperate too, and I thought that if I could just touch his clothes as he walked by, that would be enough. But how? Such a big crowd.

It was such a big crowd – and they were all coming too. I wished they wouldn't. We would be there so much faster without all these people. Inside I was screaming for them to go away.

"Go away! Get back inside away from decent people!"

People were shouting at me, but this time I wasn't going to take any notice. I kept going – into the crowd, closer and closer to Jesus. But I couldn't get close enough, there were just too many people and I wasn't strong enough to push my way through them. I could feel my excitement turning into despair, but then I looked down, and there it was – the edge of his cloak right in front of me. I leaned forward and reached out my arm as far as I could, and then I felt it- I felt the material brush past my fingers. And then, the most amazing feeling. I can't describe it but it swept through the whole of my body and I knew, I just knew I was healed.

I tried to make my way out of the crowd, but then Jesus stopped.

Oh no, please don't stop! Why has he stopped? What's happening?

"Who touched me?" he said. One of his friends said, "There's a crowd of people all round you, what do you mean?" I breathed a sigh and looked for a way out of the crowd.

He was still not moving, and then he spoke again, "Someone touched me - power has gone from me." And then this woman came from nowhere and fell at his feet and told him it was her.

'Ok, so that's that – now you know' I thought. 'Now we can keep going – please.' But he didn't move; he was totally focused on this woman now, and she was telling her life story – how she'd been bleeding for twelve years and the loneliness of it all. It seemed like an eternity. And then Jesus spoke.

"Daughter, your faith has healed you, Go in peace."

"Daughter, go in peace."

'Your daughter is dead, master I'm so sorry, your daughter is dead.' It was like a bad dream. One minute I'm seeing this woman healed before my eyes, and then my servant is here saying my daughter is dead; it's too late! No need to bother the teacher any more. I sank to my knees. Apart from the massive knot in my stomach, I felt numb. I didn't know where to turn. I looked up in desperation and my eyes met his. "Don't be afraid," he said, "just have faith, and she will be healed."

Daughter, your faith has healed you. Go in peace.

And so on we walked. And still the crowd would not leave us alone. My head was raging, and yet I was clinging on to something. Jesus was still telling me to have faith, and in my mind I could still see the face of that woman as he spoke to her.

Daughter, your faith has healed you. Go in peace.

At last we were at home. The mourners were there, wailing. Jesus told them to stop. He said that my daughter was just sleeping. And then he took me and my wife and three of his friends into the room where she lay. As I saw her lifeless body, I fell to my knees again and wept. But Jesus took her by the hand and said, "Little girl, get up." She sat up immediately. There was that smile – lighting up that face, the smile I thought I would never see again. My darling girl, not dead, not even sick. My daughter was alive!

Later on that day Jesus gave a little girl her life back. I think he knew he had done the same for me.

THE WOMAN AT THE WELL

JOHN 4: 1-42

"Whoever drinks the water I give him, will never thirst"

He was in a bad mood as usual when I left the house. He'll be off soon I thought. He won't stick around. They never stick around. They make you feel special for a while but it doesn't last. No – it's not all their fault. It's mine as well. I find myself winding men up deliberately, daring them to go and, in the end, they do. So what's that about- boredom? Fear of getting too close? I don't know. But I do know the special feeling never lasts.

So I made my way towards the well with my water jug. It was so hot, always is at midday, but I can't go any other time – too many people about – making judgements. Do I need to feel any worse than I do already?

But today as I approached the well I could see that I was not going to be alone. There was a man there. Shame. Mentally I braced myself for some kind of verbal attack, but as I got closer, I realised he wasn't from our town. In fact, he was a Jew! What on earth was he doing here? Well, at least he knew nothing about me. And at least there would be no conversation. Jews do not speak to Samaritans.

But I was wrong. He did speak to me. He asked me for a drink. That knocked me back a bit. I wasn't sure how to respond. But there was nothing accusing about him, and it felt good to be asked for help. I wanted to know more; why was he talking to me, a Samaritan woman? So I asked him, and then he said that if I knew who he was, I would be asking him for living water.

Well, I was really curious now. Who was he? I wanted him to say more and we were sitting at Jacob's well, so I said; "Are you greater than our father Jacob?"

He didn't say yes or no but went back to the water theme, which was clearly important to him. He said that he had water that would mean never being thirsty again. Oh, that sounded good, that sounded so good, the thought of not dragging myself to the well every day in the heat. And then there something in his voice, something that sounded like concern and compassion. I hadn't heard that tone of voice for a long time. So I asked him for this water, whatever it was. And then those words.

"Go and get your husband," he said.

Here we go, here comes the condemnation! I could have lied, but somehow I didn't want to. He was sincere so I wanted to be too.

"I have no husband," I said.

"You are right," he said, "for although you have had five husbands, the man you are with now is not your husband."

There it was, out of the blue! A complete stranger, laying my life before me! He knew me! How did he know? Who was he? But again there was no condemnation. There was warmth in those eyes. There was love in those eyes. And then for some reason I was on the defensive again, doing what I always do with men, pushing them away, pointing out our differences.

"We worship on the mountain," I said; "you worship in the temple."

"A time is coming," he said, "when true worshippers will worship the Father in spirit and in truth."

'A time is coming.' So this man was a prophet then.

"I know the Messiah is coming," I said, "he will answer all our questions. He can save someone like me."

"That is who I am," he said; " I who speak to you."

And suddenly, after years of rejection, I felt special again. I felt like he had been waiting for me. He had put himself in a place where he could have been rejected, right in the middle of Samaria, so he could speak to me. I could not keep that to myself, so I gave him one last look and ran back to the town. Now I want to be seen. I want everyone to come and see this man who knows me, everything about me, and loves, yes loves me anyway- and offers me living water.

So come, come to him! Come as you are, come.

BARTIMAEUS

MARK 10: 46-52

*A blind beggar by the name of Bartimaeus,
son of Timaeus was sitting beside the road.*

I can't remember when I last felt that excited. Jesus was in Jericho and on his way to Jerusalem. I was determined that I would go with him all the way. The significance of this journey was all I could think about. At last, the end of Roman domination. Jesus was going to Jerusalem to save his people, I was sure of it. This was no ordinary man. He was special. The miracles have proved that. I couldn't wait to get to Jerusalem!

And I wasn't the only one. There were so many in this crowd, wanting to make this journey with him. I was determined to stay as close to him as possible. I wanted to hear what he was saying, I wanted to hang on every word.

Soon we reached the outskirts of the city. This was the worst place. 'Won't be sorry to get through this,' I thought, 'it stinks!' Rubbish, rotting food, beggars – what a combination. We crowded round Jesus to protect him from the polluted atmosphere and hurried the pace on a little bit.

But then there was this huge cry coming from the side of the road, from the middle of a pile of rubble.

"Jesus, son of David, have mercy on me!" and then again, "Have mercy on me, Son of David!"

Oh, it was a pitiful wail. 'Even more reason to push on,' I thought.

I hoped Jesus hadn't heard, but then the beggar wailed again,

"Jesus son of David, have mercy on me!"

I looked round at him. What a sight this man was! He was obviously blind – his arms were flailing in the air – desperately reaching out towards someone he couldn't see. I was irritated now. This was a distraction we could do without. Did this man not know how important Jesus was, and what he was about to do? Some of us shouted at him to be quiet but he took no notice – he just kept crying out. I was furious now!

"Leave Jesus alone!" I screamed.

But inevitably the noise got through to Jesus and he stopped.

"Call him," he said.

This is what I'd feared. Jesus was such a good man. He had healed so many poor, wretched people, just like this blind man. Looks like he was going to do it again – but on such a day as this? Why can't he get his priorities right?

Resentfully, we called to the man,

"Come on then, cheer up – you've got what you wanted.
He's calling you. Quickly come!"

Oh, he was quick alright. He jumped up, threw off his cloak and ran over. The crowd made way for him. Some, I noticed, were encouraging him. Some were holding their noses.

"What do you want me to do for you?" Jesus said.

'Strange question' I thought, but to be honest, I couldn't help be moved by what happened next.

"I want to see," the blind man said.

'What now?' I thought. 'Are you going to rub dirt in his eyes? Pray over him – what?'

Just six words in the end- "Go, your faith has healed you."

From where I was I could see the blind man's face very clearly, and watching the transformation in his eyes was incredible. Suddenly the rest of the crowd evaporated. It was just Jesus and the blind man, face to face; eyes once sightless, meeting those eyes of compassion. And joy, yes real joy in both. In that moment Jerusalem seemed to be forgotten. I suddenly got it. Jerusalem was forgotten for now. Right now, Jerusalem wasn't important.

But this man; this poor, smelly, now jumping-for-joy man – this man was.

UP ON THE ROOF

MARK 2: 1-12

*When Jesus saw their faith, he said to the paralytic,
"Son, your sins are forgiven."*

To be honest, I was taken aback at Thomas and his insistence that we take Bart to Jesus. I guess I had just got used to Bart being the way he was. He had always been the way he was, right from birth. We had grown up together, all five of us. It was a tight community our village – well, most of it anyway. Not everyone. There were the odd few who never gave Bart the time of day – blamed his disability on his parents. They must be sinners apparently. 'No more than anyone else,' I thought. It was the same for Simeon and Thaddeus too. We grew up knowing that Bart was a bit different – he couldn't get up and walk.

His father had to carry him around when he was young, but his father was dead now, and Bart was bigger and heavier. So we took over, me and the boys. We took a corner of his mat and took him out, normally to Galilee. He loved the lake, so we would sit by it and share stories. Shared the bad stuff too. When one of you is so obviously weakened it seems to make it ok for the rest of us to be weak too, so we were quite open about the stuff that was getting us down. Well, not Timothy so much. He's the upbeat 'I can do anything' type of guy – good to have around when there's a big challenge – not so good if you're down and you just want someone to moan to.

Thomas is the creative one, the ideas man. And Simeon – he's the practical one. He's the one that can take Thomas' ideas and actually make them work. He's not all bluster and brawn; he actually knows what he's doing. Then there's Thad. He's a thinker, a reader, very wise and spiritual – slightly pessimistic. And I'm John. I'm a fisherman. I love the water. I love to take Bart out in my boat.

In fact I was just bringing the boat in with Bart when I saw Thomas on the shore waving frantically. He rushed down to help me pull the boat in.

"Jesus is in town," he cried, "he's in one of the Pharisees' houses – just down the road – we need to get Bart to him. He healed loads of people last time he was here."

I looked at Bart. He was looking confused.

"I'm not sure Thomas," said Bart. "He's with the Pharisees – it's probably important stuff going on there."

"Rubbish – let's get the other two. What's more important than this?"

Thad and Simeon thought it was worth a shot – so we each took a corner and walked down the street towards the house.

That's when reality hit. There was a massive crowd outside the door. Obviously the Pharisee's house was full to bursting and people were congregating outside the door, trying to catch the odd word of what was being said inside.

"We're never going to make it to Jesus," said Thad. "This is hopeless. Maybe we can come back in a couple of hours and see if he's still here and some of the crowds have gone."

"Rubbish!" said Thomas, "we'll do this now! Let's get up on the roof."

And for some reason that none of us understood, we were following him up the outside staircase to the roof.

"Ok, so now what?" I said. "Lovely view and all that, but we're up here and Jesus is down there."

"We'll have to go through the roof."

"That's not going to go down well with the owner," said Thad.

"Not bothered too much about that, Thad; we'll just take some of this roof matting up and lower him down."

"With what?" said Thad; "our arms aren't that long."

"You're right, we need rope. John, you must have some."

Yes, of course I had some rope. So I ran off back home to get as much as I could find. None of the people outside the house seemed remotely interested in what we were doing. 'Just as well,' I thought, 'this was breaking and entering in a big way'.

I could hear Jesus' voice. It was muffled and I couldn't hear the words, but it was a voice of authority. No-one was questioning what he was saying.

We started to pull away at the layers of reeds and branches that made up the roof. I had been caught up with Thomas' enthusiasm, but now doubts started to enter my mind. What if Jesus didn't like being interrupted? What if the crowd got angry in there and assaulted Bart as we lowered him? What if the rope didn't hold and we dropped the poor guy? I looked at Bart. Surely the same thoughts were going through his head – but he didn't show it. He watched us working away at the roof, with complete trust in his eyes. This was a big risk for him, but he trusted us. I loved him even more for that.

Eventually the hole was big enough for Bart's mat. We attached the rope and started to lower him. Jesus had stopped talking now. He was looking up. We held the ropes steady and Bart went lower and lower. There was considerable pain in my arm and, I'm guessing, all the others too, but it was overtaken by the sense of anticipation of what could happen here today.

Jesus' eyes went from one of us to the other. All four of us were taken in and then, such a sense of relief. If Jesus didn't like being interrupted, he had a strange way of showing it – because he beamed at us. And then he looked down – he looked at Bart and said the strangest thing, "My son, your sins are forgiven."

Not quite the words we were looking for, and for a while my heart sank. The Pharisees started to mutter and grumble. Simeon whispered to me, "What is he saying? Only God can say that!" I think the Pharisees were saying the same thing, but not the way Simeon was. He was excited and in awe – these people were incensed! Jesus then said,

"Which is easier? To say your sins are forgiven, or to get up and walk? This is to show you that the Son of Man has the authority on earth to forgive sins."

And then came the moment of magic. He turned to Bart again and said,

"Take up your mat and walk."

And he did. Bart got up – for the first time in his life.

There was a gasp in the room – there was a gasp on the roof. The rope ends dropped from our hands. We wouldn't be needing those again. We screamed with delight and then ran down the stairs to meet our friend who was walking, yes walking, through the door.

THE WIDOW
OF NAIN

LUKE 7: 11- 17

When the Lord saw her, his heart went out to her

I remember thinking, 'Why does there have to be a procession? Why do I have to bear my grief so publicly?' It was bad enough when my husband died two years ago, but this was my son, Matthew, my only son, lying lifeless in that coffin. I just wanted to shut myself away and cry and cry until there were no tears left. But that's not the way we do things. There has to be a procession. So we made our way, the crowd and me, towards the city gates.

It seems ungrateful to wish they were all somewhere else; after all, I was going to need their support. The two men in my life were both dead. My husband passed away after a long-term illness and Matthew died of a fever – no warning. One day he was fine, the next he was sick, and the morning after that, he was dead. I had prayed all through the night, but there was no answer from God. Matthew breathed his last as the sun rose, and now all I wanted was for my life to be over as well.

These were the thoughts that filled my head as I walked down those streets, surrounded by people who meant so well. I had lost my husband and my son, and with them went my livelihood. I could not inherit the farm, being a woman and if I could, who was there to work the land? I was facing a life dependent on charity from those good people who now surrounded me.

As we headed towards the city gate, I couldn't help remembering the days when they were both alive. How close we were! I had only been able to bear one child so Matthew was our world. He wasn't a perfect child by any means, but he grew into such a fine man and I was so proud, proud of them both. Two more hard-working men you could not find anywhere. And they always let me know how much they loved me. I was never taken for granted, and though I had not been blessed with many children like so many are, I felt like the luckiest woman alive. I remember praising God every morning and every evening.

So why had he taken them from me? In the space of two years, my world had fallen apart. Here I was, surrounded by people, all being so kind and compassionate, but I had never felt so alone, and the tears began to stream down my face.

We were nearly at the gate now, and the noise was increasing. I raised my head and realised there was another procession coming the other way. Another funeral perhaps? No, there was no weeping or wailing from these people. There was excitement. This was the last thing I needed. I didn't care what it was that was causing this excitement; I just wanted them to go away and for this day to be over.

But they didn't go away. Through my tears I could see that a few people from this crowd were making their way towards me. 'They are joining our procession out of respect,' I thought to myself. I tried to smile and acknowledge their kindness but a smile just wouldn't come and I bowed my head and sobbed helplessly.

I don't know how long I was crying but when I looked up again, there was a man standing right next to the coffin. His eyes were fixed on me, and as my vision became clearer I saw that his eyes were shining with tears. Did he know my son? No, this was a stranger, and yet I could see pain in his face. "Don't weep," he said, and then he laid his hands on the coffin.

I should have been angry but I wasn't. I was transfixed now. What was he going to do?

Nothing could have prepared me for what came next. He spoke again,

"Young man, I say to you get up!"

And then, almost immediately, there he was, Matthew – sitting up in the coffin and speaking! There was no mistaking his voice. I don't know what he said, I don't care what he said. My son was alive! The next thing I remember was feeling his arms around me. And there we stood, holding each other, crushed by the crowd who started to lay their hands on Matthew just to check that he was real. All around, the weeping and wailing turned into shouts of joy and wonder.

"A great prophet has risen among us! God has come to help his people."

Some were comparing him to Elijah. And then I heard someone say the words,

"This must be Jesus of Nazareth."

Was this the name of the man who had restored my son to me? I looked around, but he was gone. I wanted to fall at his feet and thank him, but there was no opportunity for that. Instead, I closed my eyes and thanked God for sending me such a man in my darkest hour.

When I opened them, I was looking into the eyes of my son, my living son, who was smiling down at me.

He took my hand and we walked home together.

ZACCHAEUS

LUKE 19: 1-10

Zacchaeus was trying to see who Jesus was,
and was unable because of the crowd, for he was small in stature.

I thought the money would make her happy. I thought that's what all women want – nice things, nice clothes, servants to do all the hard work while they go shopping. But not my wife, Ruth. I could see she wasn't happy. I could hear she wasn't happy.

"We used to have some friends," she would say. "I used to give parties. We used to have such great parties. Where have my friends gone?"

I thought the money would make us all happy, but there were very few smiles in our house.

The money was the reason I took the job. I'm not a political animal – I just wanted an easy life really. I would leave it to the others to get angry about the Roman occupation. I didn't see that they were doing us much harm. In fact I got on well with them. So well in fact, that they offered me the job of tax collector. Well, I had never been able to make much money before and I could see there were real opportunities here. I could keep a percentage of what I took, so I soon realised that there was a fortune to be made from making sure people paid up and paid above the odds too. My wife didn't mind at first. She thought it was worth a go. But the richer we became, the less people wanted to know us. We started to argue more. And then it got even worse than that, we just didn't talk at all. She became indifferent, and the girl I fell in love with disappeared into a well of resentment. I knew something had to change, but what? If I stopped this job, no-one would give me another – I was too unpopular.

And then, as I was walking through town, I noticed there was an air of excitement about the place. Jericho was busy today. I could hear the same word being repeated over and over by the passers-by;

"Jesus is coming, Jesus the healer, the miracle man! He's just made the blind beggar see!" I heard someone say.

I wondered if he meant the blind man I have seen so often on the outskirts of our city. He's always there – has been for years. Has Jesus really restored his sight? He was the talk of the town and I really wanted to see this man who everyone seems to love. 'I wonder what that feels like,' I thought. I decided to stick around. No point in going home after all – there would be no welcome there.

However, as I waited, the crowd got bigger. I was pushed around. Nobody wanted to be near me.

"Get out of the way – you thief, you traitor!"

I'm not big enough to give as good as I get, so I was jostled further and further to the back of the crowd that was growing every minute. I would never see Jesus now – and I really wanted to –something desperate inside me was telling me that this man was important, this man was different. I felt that he could make a difference to me – how, I don't know, but I was not going back home until I had seen him.

A few yards away from me and overlooking the main route I could see the old sycamore tree. It was welcome shade from the midday sun, that tree. I had rested under it a few times myself. Today I knew I had to climb it – this was the only way I was going to see Jesus. So I edged my way towards it, and then climbed up into the tree until I found a good branch to rest on. Again, I was shouted at when people realised who it was climbing the tree.

"Pathetic!" I heard, and "Let's hope he falls!"

I held on to the branch. I was not going to fall.

Then I saw him coming. People were surrounding him on every side, anxious to talk to him. He stopped and listened. He wasn't in any hurry. He was giving everyone the time they needed. As he approached, I reflected on how different we were. He must be the most popular man in the world; everyone wanted a bit of him. All he did all day was give to people, teaching them, healing them, making them feel good. All I did all day was take from people, and now I was the most hated man in Jericho. What would Jesus want with a man like me? As he walked below I could hear him laughing with his friends and then, for no reason, he looked up and his eyes met mine. Was he going to shout at me too? No, he held my gaze and then broke into a smile of recognition. It was as if he knew I was going to be there, as if this was where we had planned to meet.

"Zacchaeus," he said, "You must come down – for I'm coming to your house today."

How did he know my name? Why did he want to come to my house? No-one comes to my house any more. Well, I wasn't going to argue. I scrambled down the tree. "This way Jesus, come this way."

All the time I was thinking, this can't be happening. He's a Jew and he's making himself impure by coming to the house of a sinner. Certainly the crowds were thinking the same thing. They were not happy. But I didn't care. Jesus was coming to my house, and with all his friends.

Ruth was perplexed but she didn't complain. In fact she was energised by the whole thing. It was some time since she had had any company and she is a wonderful hostess. So she got to work and put on a great spread. As we ate, I spoke with Jesus' friend Matthew. He had been a tax collector too, and gave it all up to follow Jesus. The loss of all that income was unimportant to him. He seemed so at peace.

And then at last, Jesus and I spoke. I thought he would say something to me about my choice of profession but the condemnation never came. He just sat and ate and talked about many things, and as he spoke I realised that the things I had thought were so important, just weren't important at all. I realised that there was absolutely no point in having a lot of money at the expense of relationships. As Jesus spoke, I felt that sense of peace that I had just seen in Matthew.

"Jesus, I am going to give half my fortune away and all those I have cheated, I will repay four times as much."

There, the commitment was made, and it felt so good. I looked at Ruth to see how she was taking it. Joy of joys, I saw a smile play around her lips. She looked happy, really happy. Now my world was complete. I searched in my head for a word to describe how this felt.

"Today, salvation has come to this house," said Jesus.

'Yes,' I thought, 'that's a good word, salvation.'

THE WOMAN CAUGHT IN ADULTERY

JOHN 8: 1-11

"If anyone of you is without sin, let him be the first to throw a stone at her"

I suppose I'd given up hope of ever finding the real thing. Men come and go. They give you a taste of happiness and then disappear. What's wrong with me? Why do they never stay? I don't generally go for married men, but Simon was different. He had status, he was in with the Pharisees and teachers of the law and when he showed an interest in me, it was exciting. At first, he would just joke with me and my sister, Sarah as he examined the fruit on our market stall. Brightened up my day. Of course, when he was with his wife, he didn't joke- he just looked.

I felt special. We became bolder. I would leave the stall just for a couple of minutes giving Sarah some excuse and we would meet in an alley – just briefly – but it was thrilling. A couple of stolen minutes soon became a couple of stolen hours.

But it always left me wanting more, and afterwards I was always left with the pain. And I found myself just waiting for the next opportunity to feel wanted. It came soon enough.

"She's staying with her mother for two days. You can come tonight."

A whole night – this was a dream. I noticed his important friends had started to notice our friendship. They would look in my direction and smile. Did they want me too?

Yes they did, but not the way I thought. That night I did go to Simon's house. It was a wonderful night. I never wanted it to end, but end it did. Early in the morning, the door burst open. Men burst in. I knew them- these were his friends. Simon was frantic.

"It's ok – relax," they said to him, "we just want her." And then, like a knife wound, I heard Simon say,

"Ok, ok – just take her! Don't say anything!"

"Don't worry, your secret is safe." Then they dragged me away.

I never hated myself more than at that moment. I was alone, special to no-one. I was going to die, in the pursuit of someone who didn't care for me at all.

I was dragged to the temple courts, a very public humiliation. My captors charged towards a group of people and then I heard them shout,

"Hey, teacher! This woman was caught in adultery! The law of Moses says she is to be stoned. What do you say?"

Then I realised what was going on. This must be Jesus. He was the miracle man, the teacher that the Pharisees hated. I could feel that hate now as they thrust me towards him. I was being used again – to catch this man out. These men were prepared to kill me to get to him.

Jesus hardly looked at me, but he looked at them, long and hard. The men around me were picking up rocks in anticipation. Jesus watched and then turned around and crouched down and started writing with his finger in the dust. Well, they were infuriated now, and just shouted louder,

"The law says she should be stoned! What do you say?"

'What would he say?' I thought.

Eventually he straightened up and turned quietly and said,

"If any one of you is without sin, let him cast the first stone." And then he just turned round again and continued writing in the dust.

Silence. Uncomfortable silence. I braced myself and waited. Who was going to throw that stone? Some of the men looked like they were going to. They passed their stone from hand to hand but they couldn't throw it. They kicked the ground with exasperation and then, I felt the grip on my arms loosen. I heard a thud of stones hitting the dust. One by one they turned and left the scene, until there was just me and the teacher, still writing in the dust.

Once again he straightened up and turned. This time he did look at me, he really looked at me.

"Where are they now? Has no one condemned you?"

"No-one, sir."

"Neither do I condemn you. Go and sin no more."

Why should he care if I sinned again? What was it to him? But I could see that he did care, just in the way that he looked at me – he really cared. This wasn't a warning that next time he may not be there to rescue me, this was real compassion that said, 'Sin no more, because whether you get caught or not, the life you live causes you too much pain. And you're worth more than that.'

THE FEEDING OF THE 5000

JOHN 6: 1-15

*"Here is a boy with five small barley loaves and two small fish,
but how far will they go among so many?"*

I woke to the sound of my aunt yelling at us to get up. We'd slept late, probably 'cos we talked so long into the night. I love these visits. Simon, my cousin, lives in Bethsaida, up in the hills, with his big brother Aaron and his mum and dad and I go and stay with him a lot – sometimes for a few days. Don't get me wrong, I love my sisters – but it's good to get away and do boy stuff. My uncle's a farmer and I really enjoy helping out in the fields.

But it was time to go home – back to Capernaum. My aunt wrapped up some left-over fish from breakfast and a few loaves and gave them to me, along with a big wet kiss.

"Here, take this for the journey," she said, "Can't have your mother saying I don't look after you."

I always enjoy this walk back home. As I make my way down the hillside there's usually hardly anyone about and I often find myself daydreaming and thinking about the fun we've had over the last few days. Today was different though. As I made my way down the hill, I realised there were crowds of people coming up from the lake, all talking excitedly. What was going on? I knew I should be getting home, but I wanted to find out what was happening. I followed the people as they made their way to a different part of the hillside, and at last I could see what the fuss was about. Up ahead of me, I could see hundreds more people all standing, listening to a man who was speaking from a rock. A woman rushed past me saying,

"There he is – there's Jesus, hurry!"

Jesus – I knew that name. Mother talks about him quite a lot at home. He's been healing a lot of people, like a doctor, but not using any medicines or potions. Mother says he just touches them or speaks to them and they are better. Mother says he's going to save us from the Romans. I'm not sure how one man can do that- the Romans are pretty scary- but mother is usually right.

I couldn't hear what he was saying, so I worked my way through the massive crowd- there must have been thousands by now- until I got a good spot not too far away from him.

I didn't understand all of what he was saying but I loved the way he was speaking- with such passion. I recognised some of his words from the scriptures that mother reads to me in the evenings sometimes. But the way he spoke was almost like he'd written the words himself. He kept talking about a kingdom, which sounded so good. No mention of getting rid of the Romans though. Maybe he'd get on to that later.

After a while some people brought their sick to him and he healed them – just like mother said. I wished she was here- she would have loved this. Thinking of her reminded me I should be getting back before it got dark.

I was starting to feel a bit hungry too, and was grateful for the fish and bread my aunt had given me. And I wasn't the only one getting hungry. I noticed there was a group of men round Jesus – his friends I think – who were getting agitated.

"We need to send these people away," one said. "It's getting late; they can get food in the surrounding villages."

I was about to go. But then Jesus spoke.

"You feed them," he said.

Well, they all had a good laugh about that. One of them said something about not being paid enough and they laughed again. But Jesus just smiled.

"Go and find out what there is," he said.

They weren't laughing any more – they realised Jesus was serious. They started to go through the crowd asking for food.

I knew I really should go home, but it was all too exciting – I just felt something was going to happen. Jesus had something in mind and I wanted to know what it was.

One of the men pushed through to where I was standing. "Do you have any food?" he asked. "Jesus needs it."

The people around me just shook their heads.

"I've got a bit," I said. "It's not much."

I wasn't even sure how much I had- my aunt had just shoved it in my hands. I unwrapped the cloth to reveal five small loaves and a couple of fish.

"You can have these," I said.

The man thanked me and took the food, signalling me to follow him.

As we reached Jesus I saw the other men he'd sent into the crowd, standing around empty handed.

"This boy has five loaves and two fish," my man said. "But what good is that among so many?"

'Yes, what good is that?' I thought, but my eyes were fixed on Jesus now. What was he going to do?

Jesus smiled. "Tell the people to sit down in groups," he said to his friends.

Off they went again- looking really fed up this time. But I felt really excited. I'd heard Jesus speak with such passion and I had seen him heal people right in front of my eyes. I felt sure something even more amazing was going to happen. What, I didn't know- maybe manna from heaven like they had when

Moses was alive. Oh yes, I've heard all about that. Mother loves that story!

Jesus raised his eyes to the sky. 'This is it,' I thought, 'manna from heaven – here it comes. Here it comes!!'

But it didn't come. Jesus wasn't waiting for something to fall from the sky. He was praying. He thanked God and then he took the loaves into his hands and started breaking them up. Then he tore up the fish and gave the pieces to his friends, telling them to give it out to the people in the crowd. They looked at him, very confused by his request and the small amount of food in their hands, but did as he'd asked.

I watched as they gave out the food, first to one group and then another but I couldn't believe what I was seeing. People were passing the bread and fish round from group to group and there was plenty of it! Everyone was eating. Then it was my turn, and I couldn't believe how much bread and fish there was- there must have been over 50 people sitting round me and we all had plenty to eat. It was really good too. Even Jesus' friends were smiling now.

'I hope they get some too,' I thought – 'they've been working very hard.'

And they did. They sat round Jesus and ate and laughed.

But their work wasn't over – when we'd all eaten our fill, Jesus told them to collect all the left-overs.

"See that nothing is wasted," he said.

Each of his friends collected a full basket of left-overs. Unbelievable – my loaves and fish feeding all those people and with plenty left over. It was starting to get dark now, and I thought again of mother and how worried she'd be. But I knew she'd forgive me when she heard my story, when she heard how my lunch fed thousands of people.

I set off with the groups of people heading back down the hill, some carrying the baskets. Jesus' friends headed off down the hill too, towards the lake. And Jesus? Well, he went the other way, further up the mountain. 'Where was he going?' I wondered; 'to find some peace and quiet maybe?'

And as for me – I ran straight home to my mother. She was a bit cross I was so late and amazed when I told her I couldn't eat any supper. My sisters didn't believe my story at all but I'm sure mother did. She made all the right noises anyway.

"Jesus didn't talk about the Romans, Mother," I said.

"Well maybe not this time," she said, "but he'll sort them out, I'm sure of it!"

I'm not so sure about that – but to be honest I don't really care. I'll let the grown-ups worry about that one.

PETER WALKS ON WATER

MATTHEW 14: 22-33

But when he saw the wind, he was afraid and, beginning to sink..

As we pushed the boat down to the water's edge my head was racing, trying to take in what had just happened. First we get the news that John the Baptist is dead – murdered by Herod. Then on top of that there are crowds of people, all wanting Jesus, and somehow he finds the energy to heal them and teach them and feed them all with some bread and fish provided by a small boy. I wanted so much to share it all with Jesus, but he needed to be alone – to pray – to grieve. So he sent us off over the lake ahead of him.

It was a lovely evening when we set off- warm balmy breezes – perfect weather really. It was a noisy boat too. So much to talk about. We were talking so much that at first we didn't notice the clouds were gathering. Darker and darker it became. And then that first rumble from the sky. The talking stopped.

I've been a fisherman all my working life. I can normally predict the weather, but I didn't see this one coming. The wind seemed to come from nowhere. Then all of a sudden the waves were breaking over the front of the boat. We tried to bail out, but the boat was becoming swamped.

The other side of the lake seemed so far away. Just trying to control the boat was taking all our energy. Time passed. It was now the early hours of the morning and we just weren't getting anywhere.

And then, there he was- the Lord! I couldn't believe it. I thought it must have been a ghost, but no, it was Jesus- walking on the water. When I saw him, nothing seemed to matter – the storm, the fact that I couldn't swim- nothing. It was Jesus and I just wanted to be with him. So I said, "Lord, if it is you, tell me to come to you."

"Come," he said.

The others muttered, "Don't be stupid!" I think some of them still thought he was a ghost.

It felt really strange at first. It was water after all, and yet I just thought, 'Jesus has said 'come' so it must be ok.' And I could see him in front of me – waiting. So I just took one step, then two, then three – and I realised my feet weren't going under the water. The water felt somehow firm. It was so strange, but exciting too!

Half way there now, and I was still feeling good. I wished Jesus was closer, but hey, I was doing it- I was walking on water. The others were still telling me to come back. I could hear my brother Andrew, and his words stung me a bit. But he's normally right about me – I do bite off more than I can chew. Why wasn't Jesus getting any closer? I took my eyes off him for just a second and looked around me.

Look at those waves! Who do I think I am? I'm not Jesus – I'm a fisherman and sensible fishermen go back to shore when the weather gets like this. Jesus still wasn't getting any nearer – in fact he seemed to be getting further away. The wind was so strong and it seemed to be pushing me back. I'm not going to make it – I'm not!!

I felt my feet go under. Oh no! So far to Jesus. So far to the boat. Should I turn back? What should I do? I could feel the water over my ankles now- then my knees. The cries of the others were getting louder. I was drowning! There was nothing I could do.

"Lord, save me!" I cried. "Save me!!"

I threw my hands up in desperation and suddenly, there it was, his hand on mine – strong, incredibly strong. It sent a pulse of power through my whole body and I was up out of the water again. Jesus supported me back to the boat. The storm still raged but it didn't matter. He was with me now.

As we got to the boat, he asked me why I had doubted. I was too tired to think about that – and feeling too much of a failure. Maybe later. Of course, as soon as we were back in the boat, the waves died down. Part of me wondered why he couldn't have done that a bit sooner.

We did talk about it later.

"You took your eyes off me," he said. "Never do that. I'm bigger than anything else you have to deal with."

Of course he's right. I've learned that lesson the hard way. But, I think I can safely say I'll never let him down again.

WALKING ON WATER (BACK TO BACK)

MATTHEW 14: 22-33

Then Peter got down out of the boat,
walked on the water and came toward Jesus.

Voice one: Peter
Voice two: Andrew

As we pushed the boat down to the water's edge my head
was racing, trying to take in what had just happened. Thousands of hungry
people on the mountainside fed by a little boy's lunch, and so much food left
over at the end. I wanted so much to share my excitement with Jesus, but I
guess he needed this time on his own.

*He wanted us to go on ahead of him over to the other side of the lake. He
must be exhausted, healing and teaching and feeding thousands of people.
And then there was that dreadful news we had, just before the crowds
arrived – his cousin, murdered by Herod. Yes – he needs time alone.*

It was a lovely evening when we set off – warm balmy breezes – perfect
weather really. It was a noisy boat too – so much to talk about- the fish and
the loaves and poor John the Baptist. We were talking so much we didn't
notice that the clouds were gathering. It was getting very dark. Then, that
first rumble from the sky. The talking stopped.

*I've been a fisherman all my working life. I can normally predict the weather.
But I didn't see this one coming. The wind seemed to come from nowhere.
Then, all of a sudden, the waves were breaking over the front of the boat. We
tried to bail out, but the boat was becoming swamped.*

We were in trouble- struggling to keep the boat upright. Exhausted and
terrified. I wasn't sure that we were going to make it. I was starting to panic –
in fact we were all panicking!

*The other side of the lake seemed so far away. Just trying to control the boat
was taking all our energy. It was now the early hours of the morning and we
just weren't getting anywhere.*

And then, there he was – the Lord! I couldn't believe it. I thought it must have
been a ghost, but no- it was Jesus, walking on the water. When I saw him,
nothing seemed to matter- the storm, the fact that I couldn't swim- nothing.
It was Jesus, and I just wanted to be with him. So I said,

"Lord, if it is you, tell me to come to you."

"Come," he said.

The others muttered, "Don't be stupid!" I think some of them still thought he
was a ghost.

*Of course we thought it was a ghost - a strange shadowy figure coming
towards us in the middle of the storm. That's all we needed! As if we didn't
have enough things to worry about – like trying to stay alive. But then Peter
shouted that it was Jesus. 'Typical! Wishful thinking,' I thought. But as the*

figure got closer, I could see that Peter was right. It was Jesus. But then of course, that wasn't enough for Peter. Here we are, about to drown, and Peter wants to get out of the boat and start walking.

It felt really strange at first. It was water after all; and yet, I just thought, Jesus has said 'come', so it must be ok. And I could see him in front of me – waiting. So I just took one step, then two, then three – and I realised my feet weren't going under the water. The water felt somehow firm. It was so weird, but so exciting too.

Unbelievably he seemed to be doing ok at first - he actually seemed to be walking on the water. I couldn't really take it in, and at the same time I was feeling angry. We needed to keep this boat upright. Peter should be back in the boat, helping us control the thing in the storm.

"You're biting off more than you can chew," I shouted.

Half way there now, and I was still feeling good. I wished Jesus was closer but hey, I was doing it- I was walking on water. The others were still telling me to come back. I could hear my brother Andrew, and his words stung me a bit. But he's normally right about me – I do bite off more than I can chew. Why wasn't Jesus getting any closer? I took my eyes off him for just a second and looked around me.

To be honest, I was also a bit annoyed with Jesus. What was he doing, encouraging him? Peter does not need any encouragement as far as stupidity is concerned! He's always rushing into things without thinking. I thought Jesus would know that by now. Why don't they both just get into the boat?

Look at those waves! Who do I think I am? I'm not Jesus – never will be!

Who does he think he is? He's not Jesus – never will be.

I'm a fisherman, and sensible fishermen go back to shore when the weather gets like this. Jesus still wasn't getting any nearer – in fact he seemed to be getting further away. The wind was so strong and it seemed to be pushing me back. I'm not going to make it – I'm not!!

He's not going to make it, he's not! He's going under! My annoyance was turning into genuine concern now. Peter is not a great swimmer. I started to shout more, "Jesus, do something!"

I felt my feet go under. Oh no, so far to Jesus – so far to the boat! Should I turn back? What should I do? I could feel the water over my ankles now- then my knees. The cries of the others were getting louder. I was drowning – there was nothing I could do. "Lord, save me, please save me!" I threw up my hands in desperation.

He really was in trouble. Come on, Jesus, do something! I know he's an idiot, but he is my brother. Just his head was visible above the water now, and then

"Lord, save me!" he cried. I saw Jesus reach out his hand and, in a matter of seconds, Peter was up and out of the water.

There it was – his hand on mine. Strong, incredibly strong! It sent a pulse of power through my whole body, and I was up out of the water again. Jesus supported me back to the boat. The storm still raged but it didn't matter; he was with me now.

As I watched them walking back to the boat, I felt such relief, and then the relief started to turn to something else. What was it? Envy I think, yes, envy. My brother was walking on the water with Jesus. What must that feel like?

As we got to the boat he asked me why I had doubted. I was too tired to think about that – and feeling too much of a failure. Maybe later. Of course, as soon as we were back in the boat, the waves died down. Part of me wondered why he couldn't have done that a bit sooner.

As soon as they were back in the boat, the waves died down. 'Why couldn't he have done that sooner?' I thought.

We talked about it later. "You took your eyes off me," he said. "Never do that. I'm bigger than anything else you have to deal with." Of course he's right. I've learned that lesson the hard way. But, I think I can safely say, I'll never let him down again.

MONOLOGUES FOR
HOLY WEEK
AND EASTER

MARY MAKES BREAD

LUKE 2: 34- 35

*This child is destined to cause the falling and rising of many in israel,
and to be a sign that will be spoken against, so the thoughts of many
hearts will be revealed. And a sword will pierce your own soul too.*

(Mary is kneading dough)

Yes, my love, I'm making bread again. Well, the neighbours are eating with me tonight and there is much to do. Your brothers and sisters will be here too – and oh yes, I've invited Zebedee- and his wife. I really must try and get on with her, because I know how much her sons, James and John, mean to you. But it's difficult – she is so full of herself!

Ah, but I do love to give a party. And I love making bread. It takes time- and I love that. It takes energy and effort – and I love that too. It reminds me of a time when I had some control- before I had to let you go.

When you were little, you used to sit and watch me as I worked. I would work away at the dough and you would talk – of many things- normal boy stuff as well as higher spiritual things. Yes, the human and the divine were both there – right before my eyes- even then.

Then when you were grown up, you would work away at a table or a chair as I worked away at the bread. And still we would talk – about good and bad- your growing desire to serve. You couldn't hide your excitement when you knew your time was coming. And then, when your dear father died, we would talk away our grief. You were such a comfort to me then.

So now I still talk to you as I make bread. Foolishly perhaps, I imagine you listening, somewhere. I don't see you much now, you have so much to do; and I wonder if you ever think of home, if you ever think of me, making bread.

You did say once, that when you were out in the wilderness, looking at the rocks around you and feeling the ache in your stomach, all you could think about was my bread.

I wonder, did you think of me, when you took those five loaves into your hands on that mountainside full of hungry people?

Do you have time to think of me at all? Maybe not – but I'm still your mother. And I know there is much to be done, and there is so much need around you, and your heavenly father can meet all your needs. But I'm still your mother, and if you were here now, I'd tell you to be careful. I'd tell you to watch out for those people, powerful people, who resent you and the attention you are getting. They want to harm you, I'm sure of it. Be careful, my love.

That's not all I'd say, though. I'd tell you how proud I was too; proud of the man that you are- a man who can resist the devil with a word of scripture, a man who offers comfort and healing with a touch or a word, and who can feed a multitude, just by breaking bread.

There, this is ready I think. And I'm ready too. Tonight, there will be no need for you to increase the food supply or turn water into wine. It's your presence I will miss, not your miracles.

MARY AND THE MOTHER OF THE THIEF ON THE CROSS
(BACK TO BACK)

LUKE 23: 32-43

When they came to a place they called the skull, there they crucified him, along with the criminals - one on his right, the other on his left.

Voice one: Mary
Voice two: Mother of the thief

Yes my love, I'm making bread again. We're back in Jerusalem for Passover. You are here too, somewhere with your friends. You will have Passover with them, I think. You will be missed here – by me anyway. I wish I could see you.

They won't let me see you. There's no compassion for the mother of a thief. I tried my love – they wouldn't let me through. So your last days will be spent with him – your 'friend'. What comfort is he I wonder? Careless of his own life and careless of yours.

Ah, but I do love Passover. I love making the bread. It takes time, and I love that. It takes energy and effort, and I love that too. It reminds me of a time when I had some control, before I had to let you go.

I should never have let you go. You were safe here with me. But somehow I couldn't stop you. Your father had gone and part of you went with him.

When you were little you used to sit and watch me as I worked. I would work away at the dough and you would talk, of many things- normal boy stuff as well as higher spiritual things. Yes, the human and the divine were both there, right before my eyes, even then.

When you were little you would come to the synagogue. You would listen so intently and afterwards you would ask me questions and get so frustrated when I couldn't answer them. Yes, you had a temper, but you knew right from wrong.

Then, when you were grown up, you would work away at a table or a chair as I worked away at the bread. And still we would talk, about good and bad; your growing desire to serve- you couldn't hide your excitement when you knew your time was coming. And then, when your dear father died, we would talk away our grief. You were such a comfort to me then.

And when your father left us, everything changed. You had longed for his attention and his affirmation, but there was nothing in him to give. He took the easy way out and left you thinking you should do the same. You looked for someone else to impress, and he was easily found. Took you under his wing and led you down a different path of violence and stealing.

So now I still talk to you as I make bread; foolishly perhaps, I imagine you listening somewhere.

Foolishly, I would imagine you wanting to come home.

I don't see you much now – you have so much to do – and I wonder if you ever think of me, making bread.

Did you ever think of me waiting here?

You did say, when you were out in the wilderness, looking at the rocks around you and feeling the ache in your stomach, all you could think about was my bread.

Did you think of me at all out in the wilderness, with your friend, waiting for your next victims? Did you think of those days in the synagogue?

Do you have time to think of me at all –maybe not?

Are you scared – sitting there – waiting to die?

But I'm still your mother.

I'm still your mother.

And if you were here now, I'd tell you to be careful.

I'd tell you that I'm sorry for not being stronger.

I'd tell you to watch out for those people, powerful people, who resent you and the attention you are getting.

I'd tell you that it's not too late.

But I'd tell you how proud I was too – proud of the man you are.

I'd tell you it's not too late to be the man you really are – not the one that others have made you.

A man who brings comfort and healing with a touch or a word.

A man who knows truth when he sees it.

May God protect you my love.

May God have mercy on your soul.

MARTHA
AND MARY
(BACK TO BACK)

JOHN 12: 1-11

And the house was filled with the fragrance of the perfume

Voice one: Martha
Voice two: Mary

Passover approaches and Jesus comes to us again. A special meal is called for- he smiles as I place it before him.

My heart is so full of love and gratitude and yet there is sadness in the air. I take the bottle into my hand.

My thoughts go back to another meal, not so long ago. I was so cross with Mary- she did nothing to help— just sat at his feet as she does now.

"Martha, Martha, you worry about so many things," said Jesus, "But Mary has chosen the right thing and it won't be taken away from her."

I expected Martha to be even more angry, when he said that but if anything she seemed to calm down.

It was the way he said it. No criticism- just a smile. We are different Mary & I.

I love to learn – to hear his words, I am energised by the kingdom he talks of.

I want to make sure this is a place he is comfortable in. I want to make sure he has enough to eat.

If I could, I would follow him like Peter and John and the others – but I know my place is here with my sister and brother – my dear brother. We lost him once – I don't want to be without him again.

That was the one time I was angry with Jesus – when our brother died. Why did Jesus not come to us earlier? I remember how restless I was in our house full of mourners, so I ran down the road to meet him.

I remember how numb I felt as I watched all those people weeping for my brother.

"If you had been here, this wouldn't have happened" I cried,

"If you had been here, he would still be alive ."

Again he was gentle with me. "Whoever lives and believes in me will never die – do you believe that Martha?"

"Yes, I believe," I said. "You are the Christ."

At the sight of Jesus, my numbness made way for the grief that welled up inside me. I sank to my knees and wept. And then there he was beside me on his knees, weeping too. "Where have you laid him?" he said.

"Roll the stone away, " he said.

"But the smell – he has been dead for four days," I said. He just lifted his head to heaven.

He thanked his father for always hearing him, and then, those words.

"Lazarus. Come out!"

I could hardly believe it – he was there standing before us – my brother – alive!

We stripped off the linen cloths and held him like we would never let him go.

Never let him go.

All too soon Jesus was gone with his friends, leaving us to enjoy being a family again.

And now, here he is again. But it's different this time. He is saying good bye. He is not ours to keep I know that, but there is one last thing I can do to show him my love.

I look down at my sister, once again at his feet – the empty perfume bottle at her side. I see his feet glistening with oil. The aroma that comes from them is so sweet, so beautiful.

"What a waste!" I hear a voice say "Why was the perfume not sold for the poor?"

"Leave her alone," Jesus says. "You will always have the poor among you, but you will not always have me."

You will not always have me

But because of him, we will have each other

Because of him, we have our brother

I look across at my brother and smile

I look into the eyes of my Lord

This is not the end. (both)

JUDAS

JOHN 13: 18-30

"What you are about to do, do quickly."

Am I the only one to see what's happening here?

Really? Am I the only one?

I was like them for a while-

Transfixed, hopeful, dreaming of a better world.

Hanging all my hopes on him – the carpenter from Nazareth.

Yes, people have been healed, water has turned into wine, bread has multiplied,

Exciting stuff!

But where are we going with this?

Are we any closer to freedom?

I was so optimistic, but now I'm confused.

One day, he's throwing people out of the temple, and the next he's allowing women to pour expensive oil over his feet!

What a waste!

Has it all been a waste?

"Hosanna!" they cry, "Hosanna!"

But nothing about him says to me he's going to see this through.

And all the time the people with power, real power, get angry and resentful.

And they're coming for him – I know it!

And that means they're coming for us too. They're coming for me.

Am I really the only one who can see what's happening here?

This has to stop.

It's time to look out for number one.

MARY AT THE CROSS

JOHN 19: 25- 30

Near the cross of Jesus stood his mother.

I could never have imagined it – why would I want to?

Standing in this scorching heat- helpless.

I want to run, but I can't move.

I'm supposed to protect you, but I can't even get near you.

I can only watch like everyone else.

Look what they've done to you.

My boy – hung up like meat at a butcher's; covered in blood, covered in flies,

Laughed at, shouted at- in such unbearable pain!

Oh God! How can you allow this?

Please stop it, stop it now! If you're not going to save him,
just end it now.

End this insufferable agony.

I can't take my eyes off you.

"Woman, behold your son," you said.

I behold you. I adore you, my beautiful, perfect son. My dying son.

Ah, there it is – your last cry, your last breath.

It's over, my love, it's over.

THE THIEF ON THE CROSS

LUKE 23: 32-43

"I tell you the truth, today you will be with me in Paradise."

Kept his promise he did – kept his promise. Look at this place! It's glorious! That's not a word I'm used to saying, but it is – it's glorious! Everything shines. The jewels and the gold – better, far better than anything I've ever nicked. This is the last place I thought I'd be when I woke up this morning. But here I am – because of Jesus.

Yeah, Jesus, that was his name. I'd heard it a few times before we actually met – crucified next to me, he was. He was famous, he was – not as a criminal, no, not like me. He was famous for doing good stuff, you know, healing, teaching and that – miracle man, he was.

I have no idea how he ended up on that cross, except that the crowd wanted it. That crowd was ugly, baying for blood it was; and this is the bit I couldn't believe- they let Barabbas go. Pilate gives them the choice- to release Jesus or Barabbas and they choose Barabbas! Now he's real low life he is, worse than me, and they let him go and put this man to death. He never stole anything, he never beat anyone up or killed anyone, but they wanted him dead. That makes no sense. And not only that, as they were banging in the nails and laughing at him, he's saying, "Father, forgive them." Forgive them! These men, gambling over his clothes and stuffing vinegar in his mouth! He wants his father to forgive them? I'm not sure any father could do that.

Don't get me wrong, not everyone wanted him dead. There were a few standing a way off, weeping. One of them was his mother- pretty sure about that. He talked to her from time to time, making sure she was alright. Don't reckon she was, watching her son die like that – no, she was far from alright. Made me glad my mother wasn't there. She passed on years ago. Yeah, I'm glad she didn't live to suffer the grief I would have given her.

The sky was getting blacker now and Jesus was getting agitated. I could see he hadn't got long to go. There was another matey on the other cross - real hard nut he was and he was giving Jesus a hard time over the other side. As bad as the crowd, he was, taunting him.

"Why don't you save yourself and us?" he cried.

I'd had enough, and I shouted at him to have some respect. That's another word I don't use very much, but there was something about Jesus that brought that out of me. There was a sign on Jesus' cross that Pilate had written, 'King of the Jews' it said. Maybe that was the only thing Pilate got right that day. Maybe this man was a king. And before I knew what I was doing I heard these words coming out of my own mouth,

"Jesus, remember me when you come into your kingdom."

He was nearly dead now – hardly had the strength to look at me, but he did all the same. He really looked at me. I'm sure he was trying to smile.

"This day," he said, "this day, you will be with me in Paradise."

Not long after that he gave one last almighty cry, and then he was gone. Gone to his kingdom – and like I say, he kept his promise too, 'cos here I am as well. One day, maybe someone will explain why Jesus had to go through all that pain. And one day, maybe someone can explain why he ever left this beautiful place. It really is something, but do you know what? These jewels, and all this gold, it's nice, it's very nice, but there's real treasure here, and I'm about to spend eternity with him.

MARY MAGDALENE AT THE TOMB

JOHN 20: 10- 18

"They have taken my Lord away, and I don't know where they have put him."

There were angels here. At least I think there were. Maybe my mind is playing tricks with me again. Maybe it was just a dream. But I saw them and heard them- angels in white, sitting where my Lord should have been resting in peace.

"Why are you crying? " they said.

Why was I crying? What else could I do? My Lord was dead, and now someone had taken him from his tomb. And now I'm thinking it must have been a dream because as I look into the tomb again, there is nothing but darkness.

I am alone again. I was hoping Peter and John would help me find him. That's why I went to them. And they did come; and they saw what I had seen earlier- the strips of linen that they had wrapped him in and the burial cloth that had covered his head, still there in the tomb. But Jesus was gone. I don't understand. And now Peter and John have gone too. They went back to tell the others that someone has stolen my Lord. Why? Why would they take him? They've got what they wanted – he's dead! Why can't we at least have somewhere to mourn. There is such a pain inside me and it won't go away.

I would have followed him anywhere, this man of God, who gave me a second chance. I was out of control when he found me. Something had taken hold of my head and I couldn't do anything about it. I had no peace, I couldn't function. The words that came from my lips were evil and wild and I couldn't control them. There was no point to my existence. I just wanted to go to sleep and not wake up.

I can't remember what I was saying when I ran into Jesus – but I know it was bad. I don't know how he healed me, but I do remember the way he spoke my name, 'Mary'. So calm, so different to the way other people spoke to me. And that was all that was needed, because I felt the demons leave me. My head was clear. The tension flowed from my body. At last I could rest, I could think. I wanted to live again. I wanted to follow him, to go everywhere he went. What an adventure that was! I did love him so. I truly believed he was the son of God – the one we have been waiting for. How else could he do what he did? So many lives transformed, just like mine.

I couldn't understand why everyone didn't love him. Some people hated him. Jealousy, I think, and fear – he was becoming too popular. They couldn't catch him out so they lied about him, then they arrested and tortured him, and then they killed him. They hung him up on a cross of shame, and allowed the world to humiliate him. Nothing during my years of madness came close to that pain of watching him die, knowing there was nothing I could do to ease his suffering or that of his mother who stood beside me.

All of creation seemed to be mourning that day. I remember the sky turning black in the middle of the day and Jesus crying out to God,

"Why have you forsaken me?"

That was exactly what I was feeling. Then with another cry he was gone.

Joseph and Nicodemus buried him here. Not well enough, for now they have stolen him, leaving me as empty as this tomb.

Why am I still here? I suppose I should go. What is there to stay for? A forlorn hope that whoever has taken him will bring him back and let him rest at last. Dear God, please, please, let them bring him back.

(sound of footsteps)

Ah, at last, dear God, thank you. (she turns)

"Who's there?"

(Optional- man's voice off stage)

"Mary."

THOMAS

JOHN 20: 24- 29

"Put your finger here; see my hands.
Reach out your hand and put it into my side. Stop doubting and believe."

I suppose I should have been there; in that room with all the other disciples. We had talked about sticking together, but, to be honest, I found that really hard. Being with them just reminded me of who wasn't there – the one who had brought us together. He was dead. It was still too hard to take in and I didn't want to be around people who could talk about nothing else. The others told me not to go out. They said it was too dangerous, that I could be arrested too. But I didn't care- I just wanted to be alone with my thoughts for a while.

I reflected on the events of the day. Earlier in the morning, Mary Magdalene had come running in to say she had seen the Lord. I think we all thought that she had gone mad. She used to be mad before Jesus healed her. Maybe the shock had got to her and some of her madness had returned. She was there, standing in front of his cross; she saw him die. That's enough to unhinge anyone.

As I walked the streets, my mind went back to the time we had with Jesus. I remembered the time his good friend Lazarus became seriously ill and died and Jesus wanted to go and be with his family. This was an area where the people had tried to stone Jesus before. There was a real fear in some of them about going back there – but Jesus was determined. I was determined too. I remember I had said to the others,

"Let us go and die with him."

And I meant it too. If Jesus was going to die, what is the point of staying around. So we did go, of course. Lazarus had been dead four days when we got there, but with a word from Jesus, he was alive again.

It didn't seem possible that a man who had brought Lazarus back to life could die himself. I had always thought he would just be taken up to heaven one day when he was ready. It didn't seem to make sense that God could allow him to go through all that agony and humiliation. What was that all about? I had so many questions.

Eventually, I made my way back to the house where the other disciples were. What a commotion there was when I got inside!

"He was here," they said "We have seen the Lord!"

What in earth were they talking about? First Mary and now this. I listened as they explained to me that Jesus had just appeared in that very room. It was definitely him – he had the scars of his crucifixion on his hands and his feet.

I looked from one excited face to another. What was wrong with me? Why wasn't I excited too? They couldn't all be wrong? It must be true. And yet something inside me just wouldn't accept it. I hadn't seen him. He wasn't there now. I needed to see him for myself, so I said to them,

"Unless I see the nail marks in his hands and put my finger where the nails were, and put my hand into his side, I will not believe it."

The others just shrugged and carried on talking amongst themselves. I felt excluded, but I couldn't agree with them just to make them happy. This was too important. If Jesus really was alive, I wanted to see him myself.

"You will," said John. "He'll come back again – you'll see him tomorrow."

But he didn't come. The next day came and then the next. Some of the others seemed to be expecting him to walk in at any minute but nothing. Perhaps they were all delusional. Perhaps I was the only one with any sense.

I found myself becoming more and more of a loner that week. All the others were still talking about seeing him, but no one seemed to know where he was now. I just wanted to have some space to grieve, so I often went out alone. My thoughts strayed to the time not long ago when Jesus had talked about his death. He talked about preparing a place for us and coming back to take us with him.

"You know the way to the place I am going," he said.

I looked at the others who said nothing. Some were nodding as if they did know where he was going. But I had no idea, so I said,

"Lord, we don't know where you are going, so how can we know the way?

"I am the way, the truth and the life," he said. "No one comes to the Father except through me."

What did he mean? It was all so confusing. When was any of this going to make sense? How I longed to see some reason for his life and his death.

A whole week passed. Then the following Sunday we were all in that room again with the doors locked. Suddenly he was there. Jesus was standing among us. I don't know how; he just appeared. And in that moment I knew that Mary and the others were not mad, not delusional. This was Jesus – alive! I must have felt every emotion possible in the space of a few seconds.

"Peace be with you," he said, and then he looked straight at me.

"Put your finger here, see my hands. Reach out your hand and put it into my side. Stop doubting and believe"

I didn't need to touch anything. I fell to my knees.

"My Lord and my God!"

I was excluded no longer. Jesus, my Lord and my friend was here, with me, risen, yet still bearing the scars of death.

"Blessed are they who have not seen and yet have believed" he said.

Looking back, I realise that it was not just the words of my friends that I had doubted, it was his words as well. Many times he told us he was going to die and rise again – we just weren't listening properly. I wish I had really understood what he was saying.

One thing I don't regret is wanting to see him again for myself. That was the most wonderful moment I will ever experience and I can't wait to tell 'those who have not seen' all about it.

BREAKFAST ON THE BEACH

JOHN 21: 1- 19

"Simon, son of John, do you love me?"

Sometimes I wondered why he bothered to change my name. What was wrong with Simon?

"You will be called Cephas," he said.

He was calling me Peter- the rock. Of all his disciples, why did he give me that name? I couldn't think of anyone who was less rock-like. Stable and firm? That just wasn't me. I was always doing the wrong thing, saying the wrong thing. He was always correcting me.

"Get behind me Satan," he said when I questioned him talking about his death. He was right though; he was going to die. I just wasn't listening.

I didn't want to listen. This man had changed my world. Life was so exciting. Each day was full of wonder – the miracles and healings, even the dead raised to life; and his teaching was captivating. He had the words of eternal life. No, I didn't want to listen when he talked about death.

I so wanted to live up to my new name and be the rock he needed me to be. I remember the excitement of stepping out of that boat in the storm and walking on the water towards him. But of course, I took my eyes off him, and I would have drowned had it not been for that strong arm pulling me out of the water.

"You of little faith, why did you doubt?" he said.

Not very rock-like. And certainly not in Gethsemane.

"Stay awake and watch with me," he said. He knew what was coming – but me, I was still blind, refusing to think the worst could happen. Yes I was tired, but why could I not have stayed awake? I was supposed to have been his rock. And then came Judas and that kiss. Why, Judas, why? I was so shocked by his betrayal and so helpless when faced with all those soldiers- so what do I do? I cut off a man's ear! How was that going to help? And Jesus, what does he do? They're dragging him away, and he still finds the compassion to heal the man that I've wounded.

And my greatest failure? That was still to come, and he knew it.

"Even if all the others desert you, I never will," I said.

"Before the cock crows, you will deny me three times," he said.

And gripped by fear and disappointment and confusion, that is exactly what I did in that courtyard. In the distance I could see Jesus being questioned. Then suddenly I was being questioned too:

"Aren't you one of them?"

"I'm sure I've seen you with him."

"Wasn't that you in the olive grove?"

"No, it wasn't! That wasn't me! I don't know the man!"

And then the cock crowed, and his eyes met mine. That was too much to bear. I had to get away. I have never wept the way I wept that night. Surely this was a bad dream! This couldn't be happening. He called me Peter- his rock.

But it was real. They killed him. John saw it happen. My shame wouldn't let me go anywhere near the cross. Then they took him down and buried him.

But this was Jesus, son of God, who had already shown he has power over death. Sunday came – that glorious day – and there he was, alive among us, still bearing the marks of crucifixion, holes in his feet, hands and side.

He told us he was sending us out. Maybe the others, but not me. No, I had proved that I didn't have what it takes. Best to go back to what I know – fishing. It's a good profession and I have a family to support.

But this morning, it wasn't going so well. John and James were with me, like the old days. But we had caught nothing overnight. As we came back to shore, we saw a man cooking on the beach.

"Put your nets down on the right hand side of the boat," he said.

We did as we were told. We thought the nets might break with the huge amount of fish we caught. This had happened before.

"It's the Lord," said John.

I was out of the boat again – striding towards the shore. Despite the feelings of guilt that wouldn't go away, Jesus always brought out that reaction in me. I just wanted to get to him. The others hauled in the catch and we sat down to eat together.

But for me, it wasn't the same as before. I still couldn't shift the guilt of letting my Lord down when he needed me most. I ate a bit, but I had no appetite. I needed to get away again, so I made an excuse about checking the nets for holes and left them talking.

Minutes later, Jesus was there beside me.

"Simon, son of John, do you truly love me more than these?"

No Peter this time, no mention of rocks. He was talking to Simon, the fisherman, the man I was that day I decided to follow him, after that first miraculous catch of fish.

"Yes Lord, you know that I love you."

"Feed my lambs."

"Simon, son of John, do you truly love me?"

"Yes Lord, you know that I love you."

"Take care of my sheep."

"Simon, son of John, do you love me?"

I could hear my voice breaking up as I answered for the third time,

"Lord, you know all things, you know that I love you."

"Feed my sheep."

Yes, he knew that I loved him, but he knew that I needed to say it. As I declared my love for him, I felt the knot in my stomach unravel.

I don't know how long he will be with us this time – maybe not too long. I think he is anxious to be with his Father again. But he has a job for me to do. Where will the journey take me this time? I don't know, but I will follow him – all the way to a cross if necessary.

Where else can I go? He has the words of eternal life.

Mosaic Creative

We are a small training consultancy, specialising in the use of drama, cartoons and illustrations to enhance learning and development. Our approach is about provoking a reaction, communicating ideas, exploring meaning and unlocking the creative potential in others.

Jackie Mouradian

Jackie is a professional actor, script writer and facilitator, working with both the corporate and charity sectors, especially in the context of organisational change and development. She writes and performs in sketches relevant to the needs of the company or organisation. She also co-writes community development materials for use in urban priority areas in the UK as well as communities overseas.

Bill Crooks

Bill has worked with the not for profit sector for over 30 years, both in this country and overseas, running courses on a wide range of community development issues. He is an accomplished cartoonist and illustrator and uses these skills to powerful effect in his training courses and workshops. He has been involved in the use of the performing arts in training and facilitation for the last 10 years.

mosaic creative

Tel: 0118 9611359

Email: bill@mosaiccreative.co.uk

www.mosaiccreative.co.uk